AF480831

THINKING MACHINES: DEMYSTIFYING ARTIFICIAL INTELLIGENCE

SHORT BOOK ON AN INSIDE LOOK AT THE AI TECHNOLOGIES AROUND US

DR. SHAHRUKH KHAN

In the name of God, Most Gracious, Most Merciful

This book is dedicated to my family - my beloved parents, Adv. Mohd Saghir Khan and Smt. Shahnaz Khan and my cherished sister, Dr. Sharika Khan.

Dad, you are my hero. Your unwavering integrity, wisdom and dedication have been my infinite source of inspiration. You taught me the true meaning of perseverance, humility and strength of character through your own life's example. Any good I do is a credit to you. I would not be the man I am today without your guidance.

Mom, you are the heart of our family. Your endless love and nurturing allowed me to dream big but stay grounded. You encouraged me to reach for the stars while instilling solid values. Your faith in me gave me the courage to take this leap.

Sharika, my caring sister, your passion for helping others as a doctor fills me with pride. You constantly remind me to think beyond myself and make a meaningful impact on this world. Your enthusiastic support kept me going through difficulties.

To my entire family - we have been through highs and lows together. You kept me afloat through storms; you celebrated each milestone achieved. Your unwavering love and belief in me made this work possible. I am eternally grateful for the lessons learned on this incredible journey of life we share.

I dedicate this book to you all with deep affection and appreciation. You are my pillar of strength.

Contents

Foreword

We live in a world increasingly driven by artificial intelligence. It powers our smartphones, enables our virtual assistants, guides transportation, secures our networks, and drives industry advancements. But for many people, AI remains shrouded in mystery.

In this accessible yet comprehensive guidebook, Dr. Shahrukh Khan lifts the veil on artificial intelligence and gives readers the insight to engage thoughtfully with this transformative technology. He adeptly covers AI's capabilities and limitations today, grounding explanations in real-world examples rather than sensationalism. This book offers the public a practical education on a complex subject that generates excitement and apprehension.

Written from the perspective of a Practitioner and a Product Management Leader, Dr. Khan illuminates the fundamentals behind technologies that seem to operate magically at first glance. He explores the specialized nature of even the most advanced AI systems today while charting the evolution of machine-learning approaches fueling their capabilities. The book deftly balances technical concepts with considerations around ethics and the future societal impact of AI. Readers will gain a foundational grasp of artificial intelligence and an appreciation for the care and responsibility required as it increasingly shapes our collective future.

Thinking Machines provides a sorely needed primer to AI geared towards a mainstream audience. Dr. Khan manages to demystify artificial intelligence without downplaying the transformative nature of this rapidly accelerating field. His nuanced takes on the promise and peril of our AI-enabled future provide much-needed wisdom as society navigates the coming era of intelligent machines. This book will empower citizens, policymakers, and leaders to engage competently and thoughtfully on artificial intelligence and its implications for humanity.

Preface

The inspiration for this book came from a simple observation –
artificial intelligence has become deeply woven into the fabric of
our lives, yet few people truly understand it. We interact with AI-
powered technologies daily, but these "thinking machines" seem
mysterious, even ominous, to many. AI often invokes dystopian
fears of robots taking over the world. But the reality is much more
nuanced.

I became convinced that demystifying this transformative
technology for the general public is crucial. We need a pragmatic
understanding of what today's AI can and cannot do to engage
productively in its continuing emergence. AI holds tremendous
potential but brings equally great responsibility. How will we
leverage these technologies for social benefit? How can we develop
AI responsibly and ethically? I hope that this book provides
answers to such questions.

In the following pages, I aim to unveil the fundamentals
powering the AI systems many of us blindly entrust each day. You
will not become an expert but gain practical insight into how
machines can perceive, learn, reason, and solve problems within
narrow domains. We will anchor conceptual explanations in real-
world examples to build an intuition for just how specialized AI
remains today. And we will have frank discussions around
limitations, risks, and the policies required to steer innovation
toward positive ends.

I am immensely grateful to my AI practitioner and data
scientist partner, who lent their technical expertise to help create
this accessible guidebook. Their invaluable perspectives and
knowledge enabled us to demystify these complex technologies for
a mainstream audience – no math PhD required!

Think of this book as your accessible entry point to artificial
intelligence. I aim to satisfy curiosity, dispel myths, and bring
transparency to these rapidly evolving technologies. Only by

shedding light on "thinking machines" can society shape its continued development to reflect shared human values. I hope you will leave this book excited about AI's potential but equally prepared for thoughtful deliberation of its pitfalls. Let us embark on this journey to understand the machines integral to our present and future.

Acknowledgements

Writing this book has been a labour of love, and I have profound gratitude for all those who nourished me along the way.

To my brilliant partner on this journey - your technical expertise made the complex simple, but your unwavering encouragement nourished my spirit when the task seemed daunting. This book would be a shadow of itself without your passion for education and gift for clarity. From the bottom of my heart, thank you.

I sincerely appreciate the reviewers whose thoughtful feedback immeasurably strengthened this work. Your insights and critiques challenged me to sharpen each explanation and example. You helped sculpt a rough stone into a polished gem.

Thanks to my friends and colleagues who indulged me endlessly as I worked through ideas out loud. Our engaging discussions sparked moments of inspiration when the way forward seemed unclear. This book found its voice through your open ears and minds.

To my family - your love lifted me on difficult days and kept me afloat through storms. You believed in this book's purpose when I doubted myself. Your unwavering support is the bedrock upon which this work stands. I am forever grateful.

And finally, heartfelt thanks to my readers. That you have chosen to embark on this journey with me is humbling. With all my heart, I hope that the knowledge gained opens new worlds of understanding and enables you to traverse the AI landscape ahead with wisdom.

Writing this book has been a privilege. To all who accompanied me on this journey - you have my eternal appreciation and love.

Prologue

Imagine you woke up one morning and your typical routine was enabled by artificial intelligence:

Your virtual assistant cheerily reads off the day's headlines customized to your interests as you prepare for the day. In the kitchen, your smart speaker provides a minute-by-minute rundown of your schedule while the coffee maker brews a perfect cup using your preferred settings. While commuting to work, your self-driving car flawlessly navigates congested highways as you catch up on emails and news on your tablet.

You query a business intelligence platform at the office that serves up data-driven insights about current projects in seconds. Later, you brainstorm product ideas with your team and turn to an AI assistant to generate additional options based on past customer preferences and sales data. On your drive home, your car automatically routes you to the grocery store when the fridge reports running low on milk.

These glimpses illustrate just how pervasive artificial intelligence has become in contemporary life. From smart home devices to autonomous vehicles, AI technologies are becoming integrated into everyday environments and tasks. But what powers the convenient experiences described above? How do these seemingly "intelligent" machines operate behind the scenes? What abilities do they genuinely possess?

This book will help you peer behind the curtain of today's AI in an illuminating yet accessible way. We will explore the technical concepts powering different types of artificial intelligence like machine learning, neural networks, computer vision and natural language processing. By explaining how data is used to "train" AI systems, we will demystify what enables functions from digital assistants to self-driving cars.

We will use real-world examples to explore current capabilities and limitations across AI applications like computer vision, speech recognition, language translation, and more. Core themes will include appreciating the specialized nature of modern AI systems, the need for curating unbiased datasets, and why ethical oversight is crucial as these technologies advance. The goal is to satisfy curiosity, dispel misconceptions, and evaluate opportunities and risks.

Artificial intelligence will undoubtedly reshape our collective future. But societies shape the arc of technology, not the other way around. Through enlightening ourselves on the fundamentals of AI, we empower informed discussions about how to steer innovation to benefit humanity ethically. The machines of today and tomorrow need not be mysterious - let us begin demystifying the intelligence underpinning our world.

CHAPTER ONE

INTRODUCTION

Artificial intelligence (AI) has become one of the most transformational technologies of our time. AI has found its way into our smartphones, homes, vehicles, and workplaces in just the past decade. From virtual assistants like Siri to recommendation engines on Netflix and Amazon, AI already enhances many aspects of our digital lives.

The pace of advancement in artificial intelligence has been staggeringly swift. Technologies that were once only theoretical - such as self-driving cars and human-level speech recognition - are now tangible realities. So, what exactly is AI, and how does it work? What forms of machine intelligence exist today, and what abilities might emerge in the future? How will AI impact industry, society and our daily lives?

This book aims to demystify artificial intelligence for a broad readership by explaining fundamental concepts in straightforward terms. We will explore the history of AI and unpack terminology like machine learning, deep learning and neural networks. Using real-world examples, we will survey current capabilities and limitations across applications like computer vision, natural language processing and autonomous robotics.

Core themes will include an unflinching look at challenges around bias, transparency and security as AI systems become more prevalent. The book will provide practical education on AI today while discussing how society can ethically steer innovation as we advance. The goal is to satisfy curiosity, dispel hype, and have informed conversations about the present and future of thinking machines.

Artificial intelligence stands poised to be the most disruptive technology of our lifetimes. Its emergence raises essential questions about trust, accountability and the values we embed into increasingly capable machines. Our AI future need not be one of either utopia or dystopia - by illuminating these technologies today, we empower ourselves to shape them responsibly for the benefit of all. Let us begin demystifying the intelligent machines already transforming our world.

CHAPTER TWO

WHAT IS ARTIFICIAL INTELLIGENCE?

Artificial intelligence (AI) is transforming our everyday lives in ways big and small, yet confusion persists around what AI truly means. In this chapter, we will demystify AI by exploring its history, standard definitions, categories and more through relatable examples.

- A Brief History of AI

The foundations for artificial intelligence were established long before today's tech giants entered the scene. The term "artificial intelligence" was coined in 1956 at an academic research conference. These early pioneers aimed to use algorithms to solve puzzles and mathematical problems.

AI research exploded in the 1960s as scientists developed programs that could replicate some aspects of human cognition. Government funding drove advances in natural language processing, knowledge representation, search algorithms and more over subsequent decades. The late 1990s and 2000s saw breakthroughs in machine learning approaches, especially neural networks modelled after the brain. The rise of big data and modern computing unlocked new AI capabilities. This set the stage for today's AI boom, powering practical applications.

So, while AI may seem like a recent advance, the building blocks have been assembled for over half a century. The technologies we take for granted, like virtual assistants, facial recognition, autonomous vehicles and more, were once merely theoretical.

- Defining Artificial Intelligence

There is no single definition of artificial intelligence agreed upon across the field. A baseline explanation is that AI seeks to automate intellectual and cognitive tasks usually performed by the human mind. The overarching goal is to create intelligent machines that can perceive the world, learn, reason about information, and take actions much as humans do.

A key distinction is between narrow or weak AI versus general or strong AI. Weak AI refers to systems focused on completing specific tasks, however complex, such as playing chess, filtering spam, or recognizing faces. General AI refers to machines possessing human-level intelligence and adaptability across different environments and problems. All the AI we interact with today is narrow.

- Understanding Artificial Intelligence Through Examples

Let's explore examples of weak AI in action:

1. Virtual assistants like Siri use speech recognition and natural language processing to understand spoken commands and generate verbal responses accordingly.
2. Facial recognition technology can identify individuals in photos by analyzing biometric facial data like distance between eyes or shapes of features.
3. Product recommendation engines learn your preferences based on browsing history and suggest purchasing using collaborative filtering algorithms.

4. Autonomous vehicles integrate computer vision, simultaneous localization and mapping (SLAM), and complex path planning to navigate environments.

In each case, the AI excels at a narrow domain but cannot broadly transfer its skills. The key is that current AI achieves intelligence through brute computational force on massive datasets rather than conceptual understanding. This makes them powerful yet fragile. Throughout this book, we will revisit the capabilities and limitations of today's AI.

- AI Subfields and Approaches

There are various types and subsets within artificial intelligence research:

1. Machine learning algorithms automatically learn and improve tasks from data without explicit programming.
2. Deep learning models like neural networks approximate human learning using many layers of connections.
3. Computer vision focuses on processing and analyzing visual data from the world.
4. Natural language processing (NLP) aims to understand and generate human languages.
5. Robotics integrates perception, learning, and reasoning to interact with the physical world.

Later chapters will provide intuitive explanations of how each subfield of AI works with examples in our everyday lives.

- The Future of Artificial Intelligence

While AI has achieved superhuman performance in narrowly defined applications, the quest for artificial general intelligence remains ongoing. Accurate, adaptable multi-domain intelligence akin to human cognition has proven challenging to engineer. Yet the rapid pace of advances suggests we are on the path to increasingly capable AI systems.

In the remainder of this book, we will unpack precisely what today's AI can and cannot do. We will pull back the curtain on technologies like machine learning while discussing opportunities to create AI responsibly for the benefit of humanity. AI is poised to be the most transformative technology of our lifetimes. By demystifying it today, we empower ourselves to shape the responsible AI systems of tomorrow.

CHAPTER THREE

THE WINDING ROAD OF AI: A HISTORICAL JOURNEY

How did artificial intelligence evolve from speculative theory to a ubiquitous reality in smartphones, homes, and workplaces?

In this chapter, we'll embark on a journey through the pioneering thinkers, technological milestones, and waves of progress that led to the age of AI we live in today. Understanding where we've been sets the stage for our future.

- The earliest stirrings: Pioneers of possibilities

While modern AI relies heavily on computing advances, visionary thinkers explored conceiving intelligence mechanically long before. In 400 BC, Aristotle contemplated syllogistic logic, now fundamental to AI. 17th-century philosopher Thomas Hobbes envisioned human reasoning as mathematical calculations. In the 1800s, Charles Babbage designed programmable analytical engines, planting seeds for modern computers.

But it was during the 1940s that theories on "thinking machines" took flight. Mathematician Alan Turing conceived the "Turing Test," asking if a computer could exhibit behaviour indistinguishable from a human. And Claude Shannon's work on information theory established key pillars of digital computing. The imaginative groundwork was being laid for artificial intelligence to take root.

- Birth of AI: Forging a new field

The summer of 1956 is widely considered the birth of AI as a formal discipline. At the Dartmouth Conference hosted by computer scientist John McCarthy, early pioneers set an agenda to make machines exhibit intelligence. The term "artificial intelligence" was coined here.

Attendees like Allen Newell, Herbert Simon, and Marvin Minsky would become icons shaping the field. They identified key focus areas like reasoning, knowledge representation, and language comprehension. The first AI labs soon sprang up at universities like Carnegie Mellon and MIT, buoyed by generous military funding during the Cold War era.

- The pioneering decades: Cycles of optimism and disillusionment

The 1960s and 70s saw massive optimism as AI research boomed. Programmes like the General Problem Solver aiming to mimic human problem-solving were developed. Joseph Weizenbaum's ELIZA chatbot introduced natural language processing. But many promises proved premature.

Government funding receded in the 1970s as limited practical applications emerged. The inability of AI to live up to lofty expectations of replicating general human cognition led to what history calls the "AI winter" - a period of reduced investment and tempered zeal.

But crucially, this time also saw steady progress in specialized domains like automated logistics and early robotics in factories. Real-world economic value for "narrow" AI was being proven despite limitations. The stage was set for the following decades once computing power caught up with ambitions.

- The knowledge age: Expert systems and statistical learning

In the 1980s, research in knowledge representation bore fruit through expert systems - AI programs codifying domain knowledge of human specialists applied in areas like medical diagnosis and geological surveys.

Simultaneously, approaches to statistical machine learning were refined. Rather than hardcoded rules, systems developed trainable mathematical models to learn from data patterns. The roots of deep learning began with neural network pioneer Geoffrey Hinton's backpropagation algorithm for adjusting network weights.

While still narrow in scope, these developments expanded capabilities beyond toy problems. The foundations for applied AI were cemented, though the computing necessities were yet to mature fully.

- The AI renaissance: When big data meets big compute

The 2000s heralded the reemergence of neural networks and immense advances in computational power and data availability. AI research again exploded on multiple fronts, from computer vision to speech recognition to robotics. Tech giants began actively acquiring AI talent, bringing academic breakthroughs to consumers.

Deep learning methods achieved human parity in tasks like image classification by crunching mountains of data on GPU clusters. AI entered the public consciousness through products like IBM's Watson winning Jeopardy! and Apple's Siri voice assistant. The AI field was energized by tangible progress after prior false starts.

- Today's AI transformation: Ubiquitous but still narrow

The convergence of mature techniques, vast datasets, and affordable parallel computing sparked today's ubiquitous AI era. Visionary founders like Geoffrey Hinton, Andrew Ng, and Demis Hassabis helped unleash AI from the lab into the real world through startups like Google Brain, DeepMind and driverless car companies.

AI evolved from an experimental academic field to a mission-critical business necessity integrated across industries within a decade. But while now pervasive, capabilities remain bounded. AI excels on narrow tasks but lacks adaptable general intelligence. The next frontiers lie in achieving transfer learning, causal reasoning, creativity and common sense - among the open grand challenges today.

- The winding path ahead

The history of AI illustrates how progress unfolds across decades through patient cumulative advances. Periods of inflated optimism often give way to discouragement before practical engineering catches up with lofty visions. We stand on the shoulders of countless pioneers, most unknown, whose bricks collectively built the foundations for AI's blossoming today.

The journey ahead remains long. But by learning from past cycles of euphoria and disillusionment, we can travel with measured hope. The winding road to truly intelligent machines calls for pragmatism, diligence and wisdom - amplifying the best of our humanity alongside the capabilities of our machines. Our AI tale remains unfinished, but its opening chapters illuminate a promising path forward.

CHAPTER FOUR

How Do Machines Learn?

For years, we've imagined having helpful robots in our homes and workplaces that can understand instructions, recognize objects and even anticipate our needs. Artificial intelligence is making this dream a reality by teaching machines how to learn. In this chapter, we'll explore how AI systems can gain new skills by learning from data to improve at specific tasks.

- What is Machine Learning?

Humans acquire new knowledge through experience and repetition. Machine learning algorithms work similarly – by looking for patterns in large datasets, an AI system can progressively improve its performance on a given task without needing to be explicitly programmed for every scenario.

For example, say we want to teach a machine to distinguish apples from oranges. Instead of hard-coding specific rules like "apples are round" and "oranges are orange," we provide hundreds or thousands of labelled images as training data. The AI looks for statistical patterns in attributes like shape, size and colour to differentiate the fruits and form its own classification rules - this is called supervised learning. With enough quality data, it learns to identify apples and oranges accurately based on characteristics human engineers may not even think to specify!

- <u>Real-World Uses of Machine Learning</u>

Every day, we interact with machine learning systems developed using these principles:

1. Facial recognition software is trained on massive datasets of human face images to learn biometric patterns unique to each person. This enables identifying people in digital photos and surveillance video.
2. Product recommendation engines on Amazon and Netflix observe your browsing and purchasing habits to predict which items you may wish to buy or watch next. The more data they collect over time, the better the suggestions become.
3. Fraud detection tools are trained on historical transaction data containing known instances of fraud to learn signals associated with malicious activity. They use this to analyze new transactions in real-time for potential fraud.

These examples demonstrate how machines can learn to excel at perceptual and analytical tasks by finding patterns in training data relevant to the problem they are trying to solve rather than requiring every rule to be coded by engineers. It's learning by example rather than programming everything explicitly. Now, let's unpack how it works under the hood...

- Critical Components of a Machine Learning System

While many complex algorithms exist, most machine-learning systems share some common attributes:

1. Training data – sufficient high-quality historical data containing examples the system needs to learn. For image recognition, this data consists of a large number of tagged images.

2. Features – parts of the data to analyze for patterns. An apple detector may consider shape, colour, and texture as a distinguishing feature.
3. Model – the learning algorithm, such as a neural network or support vector machine, that trains on features in the data to create a classification or prediction system.
4. Inference – using the trained model to make useful predictions on new future data and, for example, identifying new images with apples based on patterns from training images.
5. Feedback loop – results are evaluated to refine the model further, for example, correcting errors to improve accuracy.

Together, these components enable machines to "learn" by discovering patterns and insights from sufficient high-quality data rather than relying solely on rules explicitly programmed by engineers. Now, let's explore some common machine-learning approaches.

- Learning By Examples

Two of the most popular techniques in machine learning are supervised learning and unsupervised learning.

As the names suggest, the key difference lies in whether or not the data used for training is labelled:

1. Supervised Learning: The training data consists of labelled examples, such as images of apples and oranges with the correct fruit tagged. This allows the system to learn the relevant patterns and characteristics to distinguish between the labels correctly. Classification problems like fraud detection often rely on supervised learning.
2. Unsupervised learning: The data is unlabeled, and the system must find hidden structures and patterns independently without guidance. Clustering algorithms that automatically segment customers into groups based on attributes fall under

unsupervised learning.

3. Reinforcement learning is a third approach inspired by behavioural psychology. Here, the system interacts dynamically with an environment and learns behaviours that maximize reward or minimize penalties, like a child learning not to touch a hot stove. OpenAI's humanoid robots learn motor skills using reinforcement learning.

- Now You Try!

You want to train an AI assistant to understand spoken commands. What type of machine learning approach would be suitable? What kind of data should be used for training? Take a moment to reflect on how you would teach a machine to comprehend speech.

Later chapters will cover techniques like neural networks and natural language processing. The remainder of this book will explore specific machine learning applications like computer vision and natural language processing in greater depth. But first, let's recap the key takeaways:

- Machines can learn to perform tasks by finding patterns in training data rather than needing explicit programming.
- Real-world examples include image recognition, product recommendation, and fraud detection.
- Critical components of machine learning systems include data, feature extraction, models, inference and feedback loops.
- Supervised, unsupervised and reinforcement learning are standard techniques.

Understanding how machines learn demystifies much of the "magic" behind artificial intelligence. While the algorithms today are complex, the fundamental principles of learning through data are intuitive. In the next chapter, we'll build on this foundation and dive into the biology-inspired approach of neural networks!

CHAPTER FIVE

INTRODUCING NEURAL NETWORKS

In the last chapter, we explored how machines can learn from data. Now, let's look at neural networks - a biology-inspired technique powering some of the most impressive AI applications today, from speech recognition to self-driving cars.

- The Human Brain vs Artificial Neurons

Our brain contains a dense web of interconnected neurons communicating through electrical and chemical signals. This vast network gives the brain immense computing power. Similarly, neural networks consist of artificial neurons assembled into layers and connected by weighted links. Let's break this down step-by-step.

An artificial neuron takes in inputs, assigns importance weights to each input, performs a calculation, and outputs a value. These are aggregated and passed onto other downstream connected neurons. Each layer extracts higher-level features from the data. It sounds complex, but let's make this concrete with an example.

Say we want to identify photos with cats.

1. The input layer may analyze pixel data.
2. The first hidden layer identifies primitive shapes and edges.

3. The next layer may recognize parts like eyes, ears, and noses.
4. Finally, the output layer determines the presence of a cat by combining these hierarchical features. Each layer incrementally extracts meaningful patterns from the raw data.

By modelling the brain's interconnected architecture, neural networks can efficiently process unstructured data like images, video, audio and text. Rather than rules coded by engineers, the network learns directly from examples during training. Now, let's unpack how this training works.

- Under the Hood: How Neural Nets Learn

In training, the network is given labelled data like cat photos. It makes predictions, and errors cause adjustments to link weights through an algorithm called backpropagation. The network continuously improves with enough quality training samples until weights are tuned to extract the most salient features for accurate classification.

Once trained, the optimized neural net can recognize cats in new unseen images by applying learned feature extraction techniques. Similar principles allow for identifying faces, understanding speech, translating languages and more. Intuition may make this seem trivial, but coding these complex perceptual tasks procedurally requires immense engineering effort. Neural nets learn robust feature representations through data.

- Putting Neural Nets to Work

Thanks to growth in computation power and training data, neural networks now power many AI systems we interact with daily:

1. Facial recognition in cameras and apps uses convolutional neural networks tuned into millions of face images.

2. Voice assistants like Siri use recurrent neural nets to analyze speech, interpret requests, and generate natural responses.
3. Autonomous vehicles employ neural nets for dynamically navigating object detection, motion tracking, and path planning.

Across applications, neural networks excel at finding patterns and features in noisy, unstructured data that confound strictly rule-based approaches. Their versatility makes them a go-to machine learning approach as data and compute resources grow.

- The Next Frontier in AI

In coming years, neural networks will enable transformative applications like household robots, real-time translation, early disease detection in healthcare and more. At the same time, concerns around bias, explainability and safety must be addressed as neural nets become more ubiquitous.

Chapter 4 will build on the foundations to explore how neural networks power natural language processing. But first, let's quickly recap:

- Neural networks take inspiration from the brain's architecture of interconnected neurons.
- They learn to solve problems by example through weight adjustments vs. rigid programming.
- Applications include image recognition, speech analysis, and autonomous control.
- Concerns remain around transparency and vulnerability to bias.

Understanding neural nets demystifies the "brains" behind AI systems that keep getting smarter. In the next chapter, we'll see these principles for processing human language.

CHAPTER SIX

AI In the Real World: Robotics and Embodied Intelligence

We explored core AI techniques like machine learning and neural networks in previous chapters. But how does artificial intelligence operate when interacting with the physical rather than the digital world? The exciting field of robotics applies AI to enable mechanical agents to perceive, reason, and act within environments through embodied intelligence.

This chapter will survey critical robotics research areas and real-world applications. We'll discuss how computer vision, motion planning, grasping, and navigation empower robots to take on increasingly complex real-world tasks, from manufacturing to surgery. We'll also consider critical ethical challenges as these "social robots" enter human spaces.

- Perceiving the World: Sensing and Understanding

For robots to operate usefully in open environments, they need capabilities to perceive the world around them. Robot perception combines sensors like cameras and lidars with AI techniques like computer vision and deep learning for scene understanding.

Sensors feed spatial data to algorithms that identify objects, textures, distances, motions and more to model the environment. Deep neural networks enable detecting objects robustly, tracking their movements, and mapping spaces. With high-fidelity perception, robots can begin comprehending the world state and their position within it.

- Mapping and Navigation: Finding the Way

Perceiving static structures is one thing, but robots must also dynamically navigate environments without getting lost or colliding with obstacles. This requires continuously localizing themselves on spatial maps of places and planning optimal feasible paths.

Techniques like simultaneous localization and mapping (SLAM) fuse sensor inputs like LIDAR scans and camera images to build 3D representations of spaces incrementally. Sophisticated planning algorithms using these spatial models plot collision-free robot trajectories accounting for objects and kinematic constraints.

These mapping and navigation capabilities allow mobile robots like self-driving cars and delivery robots to travel to target destinations while avoiding hazards smoothly. However, dynamic, unpredictable environments like chaotic construction sites still challenge AI navigators. There is more research needed for robust autonomous mobility.

- Manipulating the World: Grasping and Dexterity

Mobile robots capable of travelling and avoiding hazards autonomously open many possibilities. But additional skills like dexterously manipulating objects expand applications further. Humans perform astounding feats of grasping and tool use through our hands. Endowing robot arms with similar abilities remains an open challenge.

Key research areas include tactile sensing, kinetic models, gripper design, and motion planning. Robots can achieve nuanced control to pick up, handle, and manipulate items with sufficient precision and feedback. However, reliable performance across diverse objects and conditions eludes state-of-the-art robot hands. There is still much progress needed for human-like dexterity.

- Social Intelligence: Safe Human-Robot Interaction

As robots grow ubiquitous across settings from factories to homes, thoughtfully shaping their interactions with humans becomes critical. Unlike industrial machines isolated from people, social robots require AI for natural communication, emotional perception, trust building, and ethical decision-making.

Research areas like legible motion, audible cues, non-verbal gestures, and transparent reasoning help robots collaborate fluidly with humans as peers rather than impersonal tools. However, instilling societal values into intelligent machines remains deeply challenging. Through principled design and continuous refinement responding to real-world deployment, social robots can enhance rather than replace human abilities.

- AI in the Real World: Robotics Applications

The convergence of perception, navigation, manipulation and interactive capabilities is enabling transformative robotics applications:

- Household robots like Roomba vacuum autonomously using simultaneous localization and mapping.
- Warehouse fulfilment robots speed logistics using computer vision and gripper systems.
- Robotic pharmacists dispense medications safely by manipulating pill containers.

- Autonomous vehicles like Waymo robotaxis navigate real-world roads.
- Robotic surgeons enhance precision using tremor-free manipulators and tiny cameras.
- Social robots provide educational support in classrooms through natural communication.

These examples offer a glimpse into the expanding possibilities as AI gives "brains" to mechanical bodies. But also required are ethical frameworks as these embodied agents increasingly share human spaces.

- The Future of Robotics and Embodied AI

Robotics sits at the intersection of physical and digital worlds. Mastering both domains remains complex but essential for fully realizing AI's potential. In the decades ahead, more innovative robotic development, materials science, power systems and manufacturing will unlock new horizons for mechanized labour.

But thoughtfully shaping societal adoption remains equally important. Our robotic helpers can enhance lives as collaborators through inclusive progress, elevating human dignity over efficiency alone. The path ahead will not be without obstacles, but the destination promises to be worthwhile.

Natural Language Processing (NLP)

In the last chapter, we explored the biology-inspired artificial neural networks enabling many impressive applications of AI, from image recognition to natural language processing. Now, we will dive deeper into how neural networks and machine learning are powering remarkable advances in processing human language and speech. Teaching computers to understand spoken words and textual information remains an immense challenge. But steady progress in natural language processing (NLP) brings capabilities like real-time voice translation and conversational bots closer to reality...

- Introduction

Imagine you just arrived in a foreign country and don't know the local language. How would you get around? Communicate? Order food? It would be incredibly challenging. Imagine having your portable universal translator like Star Trek to help bridge language barriers. Recent advances in natural language processing (NLP) bring this sci-fi vision closer to reality.

NLP refers to AI systems designed to understand, interpret, generate, and manipulate human languages like English, Spanish, Hindi, etc. Rather than just recognizing speech signals or decoding words, modern NLP aims to derive meaning, context, and emotional sentiment from text and spoken language. This enables translating speech or text between languages, summarizing documents, improving search relevance, powering chatbots and much more.

While early NLP systems relied on rigid linguistic rules coded by programmers, today's techniques leverage machine learning and neural networks to gain flexible language capabilities by analyzing large corpora of natural text and speech data. The results are AI assistants that can engage in impressively human-like conversations spanning multiple topics. Let's explore some key focus areas driving advancements in natural language processing.

- Speech Recognition

One longstanding goal in NLP has been developing systems that can accurately transcribe spoken language. While humans perform this effortlessly, teaching machines to convert amorphous audio signals into words and sentences reliably has proven hugely challenging. However, recent neural network-based approaches like Connectionist Temporal Classification (CTC) loss have dramatically improved speech recognition performance.

Smart Assistants like Amazon Alexa, Apple Siri and Google Assistant now routinely use speech recognition based on deep learning to accept voice commands and respond verbally. Large datasets of audio recordings with corresponding text transcriptions are used to train neural networks to identify linguistic relationships between spoken sounds and words on the fly. The models adapt to different accents, cadences and tonalities. However, some articulations and niche vocabulary still confuse them!

Real-time speech recognition lets users interact conversationally with devices and services hands-free using their voice. It powers various voice user interfaces and automated phone customer support systems. However, concerns around privacy, undetected bias and security exist regarding always-listening smart devices. Not all languages have received equal attention, with some African and Asian languages lacking speech data to train accurate recognizers.

- Text Processing and Classification

Another significant application of NLP involves processing and classifying text data. This ranges from analyzing customer surveys and social media posts to reviewing legal contracts. Companies apply NLP to derive insights from open-ended textual data across domains.

Text classification seeks to categorize documents by topic or genre. This supports applications like filtering spam emails, routing customer inquiries based on message content or archiving news articles by subject. Classification algorithms extract informative linguistic features predictive of the target classes based on training data. This works better than keyword matching, which misses semantic nuances. Continued advances in deep neural networks further improve accuracy on text classification tasks with complex taxonomies.

- Sentiment Analysis: Detecting Emotions in Text

Beyond transcribing words, NLP aims to understand human language by identifying the underlying sentiment or emotion behind texts. Sentiment analysis has applications from monitoring brand perception on social media to evaluating survey responses for companies or politicians.

Current techniques often rely on linguistic analysis to categorize the tone of written text as conveying positive, negative or neutral sentiment. Pre-defined lexicons analyze words and language patterns associated with emotions like happiness, frustration, anger, etc., to classify the overall sentiment of a passage. Results are rough but improving with neural networks trained on annotated corpora spanning diverse informal language styles and sarcasm.

However, accurately discerning sentiment and emotion solely from text remains very difficult. We express feelings in subtle, contradictory, and even sarcastic ways. The same sentence could convey entirely different emotions based on context. Understanding the nuances of human psychology through language alone represents an immense challenge for AI!

- Information Extraction and Retrieval

A primary commercial application of NLP has been improving information search and retrieval in documents, websites and databases. Rather than just keyword matching, NLP techniques can better interpret the meaning and context behind user queries and content to improve relevance. This enhances experiences on search engines and recommendation systems.

Relatedly, NLP enables structuring and extracting critical information from unstructured text documents. So-called information extraction is vital for populating knowledge bases or template data records from sources like news reports, research papers or electronic health records. Natural language processing can automatically identify references to names, dates, locations and actions described in textual content through syntax analysis to extract pertinent facts and relationships.

- Building Conversational Chatbots: The Loquacious AI Assistant

One popular application of NLP has been developing conversational chatbots and virtual assistants like Siri, Alexa, and Cortana. The goal is to enable fluid, natural-feeling dialogue between humans and machines on par with human conversation. Users should be able to chat casually with an AI assistant about their interests, ask questions, get recommendations, and accomplish tasks through casual voice or text exchanges.

This requires multiple NLP capabilities – comprehending requests, discerning meaning from context, searching for relevant information, and generating grammatically coherent responses in the user's language and tone.

Chatbots apply dialogue models comprising hierarchies of potential conversation flows, pre-defined templates, and language processing modules to mimic natural human-to-human discussion. However, most are narrow in scope and focused on specific domains like customer service. The system struggles if conversations surpass training data or require general real-world knowledge. Furthermore, they lack a deeper understanding of the topics being discussed.

Open-ended discussions spanning diverse topics, interests, and opinions, incorporating common sense, remain challenging for AI chatbots. The goal of being able to casually discuss our hobbies or family or get comfort during times of emotional need from an AI companion will require much further research!

• Machine Translation: The Universal Translator Dream

In Star Trek, a handheld "universal translator" enabled instant two-way communication between alien species by translating spoken words seamlessly. AI has made strides towards this dream through machine translation systems that automatically convert text between English, Arabic and Mandarin.

Earlier attempts relied on dictionaries of word-by-word mappings between language pairs but struggled with grammatical nuances. Modern AI translation leverages vast parallel corpora of human-translated texts to train neural machine-learning models. By studying millions of bilingual text examples, algorithms can learn to map between vocabularies and parse meaning from sentence structure.

Tools like Google Translate now provide reasonable real-time localization of websites or documents. However, accurately preserving semantics and sentiment when converting between languages with different grammar and conventions remains challenging. AI translation also risks inadvertently perpetuating cultural stereotypes found in training data. Furthermore, many rare or niche languages lack enough parallel texts to train robust systems.

While AI will gradually close the language divide, the subtleties of human meaning are often still lost in machine translation. And even human experts rarely produce perfect translations tailored to local culture! We must be wary of over-trusting imperfect systems.

- Limitations and Challenges

While NLP has progressed immensely, systems still lack the generalized language capabilities of humans that develop through years of experience. Most NLP today perform best on formal written text with clear syntax but struggle to interpret swaths of informal language littered with slang and spelling mistakes. Sarcasm and humour also confound algorithms.

Furthermore, concerns around embedded biases, privacy risks from data collection, and potential misuse of generated text exist. As large language models continue gaining skills, thoughtful oversight on ethics and objectivity is crucial. NLP should aim not just for realism in generation but responsibility.

- The Path Ahead

Natural Language Processing continues to be an immensely vibrant subfield of AI research, with developments that inch us closer to seamless speech and language understanding between humans and machines. In the coming years, we will see NLP expand into new multimodal applications combining language, vision, physical behaviours, and more to enable fluid interactions.

However, progress continues with innovations in multimodal learning, graph neural networks, and significant language models like GPT-3, GPT-4, etc. In the years ahead, we will see a proliferation of NLP applications and ethical dilemmas on the potential misuse of generative text capabilities. Instilling capacities for sound judgment and reasoning in language AI remains one of the grand challenges for the field.

But equipping AI with natural communication abilities also requires instilling capacities for reasoning, common sense, causality, and sound judgment. Safely achieving this remains one of the grand challenges in AI, requiring continued innovations and diligent oversight of ethics.

In this chapter, we explored the world of natural language processing and its subfields advancing communication between humans and AI:

- Speech recognition converts speech to text using neural networks.
- Text classification helps analyze surveys, social media posts and documents.
- Chatbots engage in conversational dialogue using context and language models.
- Machine translation bridges language divides by decoding text between languages.

While longstanding challenges around bias and meaning remain, steady progress in mimicking linguistic capabilities enables us to seamlessly integrate NLP across devices and applications in the years ahead.

In the next chapter, we will build on the AI fundamentals covered so far to survey some of the most impactful real-world applications of artificial intelligence technology across different industries, from autonomous vehicles and finance to healthcare and beyond. Understanding how AI is already transforming major sectors will allow us to have informed discussions about its continuing emergence worldwide.

CHAPTER EIGHT

AI in the Real World Today

In previous chapters, we explored the technical foundations behind artificial intelligence, like machine learning and neural networks. But textbooks only tell part of the story. To understand AI, we need to see how it transforms the world around us... This chapter will survey some of the most impactful real-world AI applications already reshaping significant industries.

- AI in Healthcare: Your Doctor, the Robot?

Imagine instantly getting a possible diagnosis just by telling a doctor your symptoms. AI is making strides towards this goal by automating the analysis of medical images, improving disease screening, and even assisting in surgery.

For instance, deep learning algorithms can be trained to analyze CT scans for early cancer detection or X-rays for signs of heart disease or fractures. By uncovering hard-to-spot patterns in thousands of images, AI augments doctors' abilities to diagnose conditions early.

Chatbots like *Ada* are used for initial patient interviews to take medical history and provide triage advice, though they have diagnostic acumen. More controversially, researchers have explored using facial analysis algorithms to aid in assessing conditions like pain, though ethical concerns around privacy and bias exist here.

Despite the hype, AI is far from replacing doctors. But it is transforming the practice of medicine by providing powerful analytical aids. The key will be ensuring human oversight and evaluating AI responsibly before full integration into clinical practice.

- AI on Wall Street: Your Robo-Advisor

From algorithmic trading platforms to personalized wealth management apps, AI and machine learning are reshaping finance. Autonomous AI trading systems now account for over half of all stock market transactions by analyzing news and market data at superhuman speeds to seize investment opportunities.

At the same time, chatbot investing advisors like Ellevest are on the rise, using NLP to understand client goals and risk appetite before providing personalized investment guidance. Machine learning algorithms crunch thousands of data points to generate suitable portfolios optimized to market conditions.

Of course, concerns persist around market instability from AI reacting rashly to news. And robo-advisors lack the human nuance needed for major life decisions around retirement or your child's college savings. As in medicine, responsible oversight and scepticism ensure AI enhances rather than displaces human expertise in finance.

- AI on the Road: The Self-Driving Car

Few AI applications generate more equal parts of excitement and apprehension than autonomous vehicles. The prospect of our cars whisking us around while we relax or work is appealing. However, handing over the wheel to an algorithm causes understandable anxiety.

Self-driving cars like *Waymo's* use a suite of AI technologies, from computer vision to spatial mapping to 360-degree perception of the environment, so they can safely navigate diverse driving scenarios. But most still struggle with unpredictable situations on chaotic roads.

While fully autonomous consumer cars remain years away, AI driver assistance tools like automatic emergency braking and lane centring are valuable steps in the interim. But tragic accidents have occurred even with backup drivers, highlighting the need to prudently assess safety before deploying autonomous systems sharing space with human drivers and pedestrians on public roads.

- AI in Cybersecurity: Combating Hackers

Cyberattacks are on the rise globally, from viruses to identity theft to election tampering. AI and machine learning are increasingly deployed to bolster digital defences and identify threats.

AI can detect subtle anomalies that signal malware or uncover fraudulent transactions by analysing massive network activity streams and endpoint data. Chatbots even interview suspected intruders! However, criminals also employ machine learning for spear phishing attacks. We are in an AI cyber arms race.

As with physical security, AI in cybersecurity should augment and empower human defenders rather than completely replace their expertise and oversight. Automated hacking countermeasures could have unintended consequences if wrongly triggered. The thoughtful governance of autonomous cyber defence systems is crucial as attacks become more sophisticated.

- AI in Your Home: The Intelligent Smart Speaker

Beyond industry, AI has also made significant inroads into our homes through intelligently automated devices and services. Smart speakers like the *Amazon Echo* with the Alexa voice assistant exemplify this consumer AI revolution.

The Echo uses speech recognition and natural language processing to accept commands, answer queries, perform tasks like setting timers or lists, and even control other smart home devices. AI recommender systems suggest customized music, products, and podcasts based on your interests. And skills are steadily expanding.

However, buggy voice recognition frustrates users at times. And many have concerns about privacy with an always-listening device. Still, when designed thoughtfully with user needs rather than as a medium for constant ads, such AI can unobtrusively enhance convenience and productivity around our homes.

- The Future of Everyday AI

This sampling of AI trends only hints at how algorithms and robots will reshape society from transportation to agriculture, criminal justice to education, and more in the coming years. Integration of applied AI into daily life is inevitable. But we must ensure development proceeds prudently and ethically.

AI should enhance human capabilities rather than entirely replace our expertise and judgment. Human values like fairness, accountability, and transparency should underpin AI systems affecting people's lives rather than inscrutable black-box algorithms amplifying societal problems like bias.

With wisdom and oversight, AI can empower us to understand our world better and address humanity's pressing challenges, from climate change to poverty. But we must remain watchful that the AI future unfolds thoughtfully for the benefit of all.

In this chapter, we explored the diverse real-world applications of AI already underway across significant industries like medicine, finance, transportation and home technology. But this is only the beginning. In the next chapter, we will look towards the future and discuss what's next for artificial intelligence as capabilities continue advancing. What new horizons will AI open up, and what steps can we take today to steer innovations in an ethical direction that enhances our world?

CHAPTER NINE

The Next Frontier of Artificial Intelligence

In previous chapters, we explored the foundations of modern artificial intelligence, from machine learning concepts to impressive applications already transforming industries. But where is it all heading next? In this chapter, let's look at the possibilities and perils of the path ahead for AI.

- Artificial General Intelligence: The Next Milestone

Today's AI excels at specialized tasks, whether identifying objects in images, translating languages, or recommending products. However, it lacks the flexible general intelligence of humans that allows adapting skills and knowledge across different environments and challenges. Developing Artificial General Intelligence (AGI) with people's perceptual and cognitive abilities remains the next grand quest.

AGI would possess multidomain expertise, common sense reasoning, planning capabilities, and social intelligence, enabling interaction with humans naturally. Such systems could revolutionize our work, discover new knowledge, solve global problems, and expand human potential. But we are still far from human-level AI. The brain's complexity evolved over millions of years, and we have only scratched the surface in mimicking it.

Some believe AGI could emerge accidentally from continued improvements to narrow AI, like more extensive neural networks. But others think new techniques, like unified architectures combining symbolic reasoning and machine learning, may be required. In any case, the unanimity is AGI research must proceed cautiously and deliberately, given the risks.

- The Labour of AI: Replacing or Augmenting Jobs?

Perhaps the most profound impact of increasingly capable AI will be transforming the labour landscape. Many routine information processing and analytical jobs could face automation by AI. However, the degree of displacement remains debated.

While AI will accomplish tasks humans perform today, it may empower us to take on new valuable creative and social roles, augmenting rather than replacing human work. However, this requires rethinking education and training programs to prepare the workforce for AI collaboration. Thoughtful policies around AI accountability and labour practices become crucial to ensuring technologies reflect shared values.

- Bias and Fairness: Ensuring Unprejudiced AI

As AI grows ubiquitous across high-stakes domains like hiring, lending, and policing, stampeding out biases becomes critical. But as AI systems train on human-generated data, they risk perpetuating and amplifying societal prejudices if not vigilantly monitored.

Researchers are exploring techniques like data balancing, bias testing suites, and algorithmic audits to uncover discrimination. Promisingly, AI itself may help remedy unfairness through pattern spotting humans miss. However, achieving fair and compassionate

AI requires acknowledging hard truths about societal injustices. Objective facts alone cannot resolve fundamental debates around values and ethics underlying so many issues of fairness or justice. However, accountable and transparent AI can aid constructive dialogue on the path ahead.

- The Neutrality of AI: Ensuring Beneficial Values

Beyond just avoiding harm, as AI systems grow more autonomous, ensuring they embody human values like dignity, truth, nonviolence, and wisdom becomes pressing. This is far more complex than adding ethics modules.

Truly aligning advanced AI with moral values requires open collaboration across disciplines beyond computer science, from philosophy and social sciences to religion and art. And cultures globally must participate in defining shared values. There are no easy technical solutions to deeply human questions of meaning and ethics. But the years ahead are critical for proactive discussions on imbuing AI with ethical purpose rather than reacting once unintended consequences emerge.

- Partners in Progress: Responsible AI Stakeholders

Guiding the continued advancement of AI for social benefit is a shared responsibility. Governments must fund research and craft balanced policies. Companies, especially tech firms, must self-regulate and democratize development. Academics and civil society groups must vigorously study the impacts on people and the environment. And all of us as citizens must thoughtfully engage to uphold human dignity.

By being judicious stewards and partners in progress, our machine creations can empower humanity to flourish at our best - with wisdom, compassion, creativity and community. While AI will challenge us in new ways, it need not threaten what we hold dear if harnessed responsibly. Our machines must reflect the better angels of our nature. And if they ever falter, may we have the courage to guide them back to our shared hopes.

The Next Chapter

In this chapter, we explored promises and concerns around the future of artificial intelligence as capabilities advance. But in the concluding chapter ahead, I will share parting thoughts on how we might thoughtfully navigate the road before us. Progress in technology is inevitable, but wisdom in wielding it remains a human choice. If we light the path with care and moral imagination, our machine aids need not travel ahead detached from human values. But nor can we relax in complacency. Staying vigilant, empathetic, and engaged is our shared duty as citizens shaped by and shaping the AI systems soon to transform society.

CHAPTER TEN

AI in Business – Preparing for the Future

In prior chapters, we explored the techniques powering artificial intelligence and its emerging applications transforming industries. But what does the rise of AI mean for business leaders? Adopting AI can enable data-driven decision-making, optimize processes, and assist employees in value-added roles. However, effectively navigating this transition requires thoughtful planning around workforce, ethics, and aligning technology with enterprise goals.

This chapter will discuss strategies for businesses starting their AI journey. We'll cover best practices around data, talent, and responsible development. And we'll highlight common pitfalls to avoid on the road to an intelligent enterprise where humans and AI collaborate seamlessly rather than compete.

- Data Readiness: Fueling AI Success

High-quality data is the lifeblood of practical AI. Unfortunately, data in business is often fragmented across siloed systems and lacks consistent formats, definitions, or context needed for robust training. Investing in an enterprise data strategy is essential before algorithms can work their magic.

Steps like migrating data to cloud warehouses, cleaning records, adding metadata, and consolidating taxonomies eliminate significant roadblocks. For many firms, the data-wrangling effort exceeds that for developing models! However, proper data foundations pay dividends as diverse business needs arise. Plus, benefits like improved reporting and compliance naturally result.

- Building vs. Buying AI: Weighing Options

With data readiness in place, companies next face build or buy decisions around AI capabilities. Creating in-house allows customization but requires specialized skills. Off-the-shelf AI-as-a-service solutions offer faster adoption with less effort but limited control.

Hybrid partnerships with AI consultancies strike a balance through domain expertise and co-creation. Either path benefits from integrating human domain experts throughout the process rather than handing off entirely to data scientists. This improves contextual relevance critical for business adoption. Change management is also crucial for smooth workflows.

- AI Talent: Developing Capabilities

Navigating the AI era requires teams blending business and technical prowess. Some roles, like data analysts and process automation, may need reskilling as tasks change. Other emerging roles like data ethicists and customer experience designers require new talent pipelines.

Educational initiatives, hands-on training, and internal mobility programs help retain and uplift workers rather than displace them. External partnerships can also fill near-term needs. However, sustaining an AI-powered business needs human capabilities nurtured with algorithmic advances.

- Avoiding Pitfalls: Prudent Perspectives

Many early AI business experiments encountered pitfalls like bias, overpromising, and lack of direction. AI is not a turnkey shortcut to business success. Setting realistic milestones, building ethics into design, and iteratively testing benefits help firms avoid inflated expectations and unintended consequences.

An outcome-driven perspective focusing first on solving business problems, not chasing technology hype, allows pragmatically uncovering suitable applications. Patience and care in deployment is critical. AI brings immense opportunities, but only as a collaborator enhancing human judgment, not an instant elixir handing firms competitive advantage overnight.

- Aligning AI with Business Strategy

AI capabilities cannot sit isolated as one-off projects but should seamlessly integrate across operations for lasting impact. This requires aligning AI roadmaps to an overarching corporate strategy tailored to an industry's dynamics.

Thoughtful frameworks on technology management help firms identify which predictive tasks, processes, and engagement models to prioritize for AI augmentation depending on strategic priorities. This helps surface high-impact AI use cases to pilot and scale based on business goals like customer intimacy, product innovation, or operational agility.

- The Intelligent Enterprise: A Future Vision

The convergence of scaled data infrastructures, responsible AI development, empowered workers, and strategic alignment enables an intelligent enterprise where humans and algorithms synergistically elevate performance:

- Agile operations through predictive demand forecasting, dynamic pricing, and prescriptive analytics.
- Delightful customer experiences using virtual agents, personalized content, and sentiment tracking.
- Innovation accelerators like accelerated R&D simulations and tailored recommendations.
- Empowered employees assisted by knowledge bots and routine automation.

This future offers ample growth opportunities across sectors. However, it requires continued diligence in navigating risks around job impacts, dependencies on opaque systems, and ethical blindspots. If pursued responsibly, AI can unlock new sources of competitive advantage and productivity gains through the augmented capabilities of both technology and people.

- The Road Ahead: A Marathon, Not A Sprint

Implementing AI across large organizations is an iterative journey, not a one-time event. Through a sustained commitment to data health, talent development, and responsible innovation, firms can continuously expand and refine areas for algorithmic augmentation. But artificial intelligence is just one component of business success. It cannot resolve strategy issues, leadership failures, or enterprise agility.

Approaching AI with sound expectations and prudent perspectives allows for harnessing its full potential. In the years ahead, the future belongs to organizations that embrace AI as an opportunity to uplift people and performance - not as a silver bullet handing competitive riches overnight.

CHAPTER ELEVEN

NAVIGATING THE DANGERS OF MORE INTELLIGENT MACHINES

The rapid advancement of AI undoubtedly brings many benefits, as we've explored in previous chapters. But alongside the possibilities sit real concerns we must confront responsibly. In this chapter, let's discuss the risks and limitations of increasingly capable AI systems so we can develop them prudently.

- The Allure of Automation: When to Keep Humans in the Loop

As pattern recognition and predictive AI prove superior to rules-based software on many tasks, there is an understandable temptation to hand over control and let algorithms run on autopilot. But entirely removing humans from the loop can be reckless if we absolve ourselves of oversight.

For example, while autonomous weapons may reduce military casualties, delegating life-and-death targeting decisions to AI raises profound ethical issues. And "lights-out" factories where machines optimize production with minimal human supervision threaten worker safety and agency.

We must carefully weigh the allure of automation against the duties of human accountability according to context. AI should not displace but rather empower human capabilities where insight and ethics remain essential. Discretionary case-by-case oversight of algorithmic systems by qualified individuals must be upheld even amid pressures for efficiency.

- Bias in, Bias out: Ensuring Fairness in AI

One limitation with significant societal implications is that AI systems often inherit and amplify biases from flawed or unrepresentative training data. For example, an HR resume screening algorithm that learns preferences against minorities from previous job records could discriminate unfairly when deployed.

We must meticulously monitor for prejudices creeping into models affecting people's lives, whether in hiring, lending, healthcare, or policing. But scrutinizing bias is hugely complex, as even data balanced across groups can propagate hidden biases through correlations. And human auditors have blindspots of their own. Promisingly, techniques in explainable AI may help shine a light on unfair model influences.

Above all, we must acknowledge that AI does not exist independent of inequities still pervading society. Fairness is not achievable by technical solutions alone but only in tandem with inclusive cultural dialogue. AI merely reflects our social mirrors - we must become more just through diversity and empathy.

- The Fragility of AI: Security and Resilience Concerns

Despite outward intelligence, even state-of-the-art AI can be surprisingly fragile. When confronted with novel inputs outside their training distributions, machine learning models often fail unpredictably. And they can be deliberately fooled by tailored adversarial data tweaks invisible to humans.

Attacks tricking autonomous systems with perturbed stop signs or bots inundated with syntax tweaks could have dire real-world consequences. As AI grows ubiquitous, enhancing security and resilience becomes imperative. A multifaceted approach of robust adversarial training, input validation, and hybrid models blending neural networks, symbolic AI, and rules-based programming may help harden systems.

But just as anti-virus software is in an arms race with evolving cyber-attacks, we may need ongoing augmentation of defences through techniques like human-in-the-loop oversight to ensure safety amid increasing AI capabilities.

- Transparent and Ethical AI: The Importance of Explainability

Most commercial AI remains shrouded under the hood as opaque black boxes providing outputs without explanations. But specifically in contexts affecting human lives, this lack of transparency creates distrust and accountability problems. Governments increasingly recognize the need for AI explainability and process logging.

The emerging field of explainable AI aims to demystify model influences and inferences by surfacing key decision factors and precedents. For example, showing how the presence of specific keywords informed credit decisions assures potential discrimination. Explainability also allows auditing and refinement of AI by human trainers. However, perfectly quantifying complex model logic poses challenges.

Above all, we must ensure AI transparency reflects ethical priorities and human values. Explanations should convey how conclusions are reached and why they are justified based on social norms. Scrutability without moral responsibility means little. Inclusive design and impact testing will be crucial to prevent explanation methods from becoming a sterile technical compliance exercise rather than proper accountability.

- Partners in Progress: Multi-stakeholder AI Ethics

There are no simple technical remedies to address the profound social impacts of increasingly intelligent and autonomous AI systems. While computing experts drive much research and development, deliberating challenges around fairness, accountability, privacy, and other issues requires including perspectives from philosophy, social sciences, policy, law, and the humanities.

And crucially, the public must have a seat at the table in charting the path ahead through participatory discourse as both AI users and citizens whose lives will be transformed. Inclusive ethical codes co-created across industries, academia and civil society provide guidance. But living up to principles requires perseverance and moral courage every day despite competing interests or incentives.

The years ahead will challenge us, but by being proactive and working earnestly as partners in progress, we can steer AI to spread new opportunities equitably while upholding human dignity and wisdom.

In this chapter, we discussed several risks and limitations requiring diligent attention as AI capabilities grow:

- Autonomous systems removing humans from the loop can be reckless without oversight.
- AI risks perpetuating harmful biases if unchecked for fairness.
- Security and robustness concerns exist around fragile machine-learning models.
- The black-box nature of AI warrants transparency for accountability.
- Multi-stakeholder collaboration on ethics and inclusion is imperative.

But technology shapes us as much as we shape it. AI risks reflect our frailties. We can develop technologies that uplift our humanity by cultivating empathy and remembering our shared hopes.

CHAPTER TWELVE

AI AND SOCIETY – CULTIVATING A JUST FUTURE

`As artificial intelligence advances, its emerging role in social institutions raises profound questions about values, ethics, and governance. While technical chapters focused on capabilities, real-world development occurs within societal contexts we must thoughtfully navigate.

This chapter will discuss urgent social questions regarding AI's impacts on people and systems. We'll explore biases, economic consequences, and philosophical perspectives on machine morality. Despite uncertainties, we'll consider pragmatic steps individuals and organizations can take today to cultivate an ethical AI future. The path ahead calls for bridge-building across sectors, cultures and disciplines to align AI with the greater good.

• Economic Impacts: Changes for Workers

One intense debate centres on AI's potential impacts on the workforce and wages. While technology has displaced specific jobs throughout history, it also creates new roles and drives economic growth. But the scale of looming disruption remains unclear.

Routine information processing tasks indeed show susceptibility for automation via AI and robotics. However, 9% to 47% of job loss estimates vary wildly based on assumptions. And macroeconomic secondary effects are complex to model.

Proactive policy, educational initiatives, employee retraining, and corporate ethics may help smooth workforce transitions ahead. But philosophical questions around sustaining meaning and livelihoods amid widespread automation warrant thoughtful public debate regardless of which projections fully materialize.

- Algorithmic Bias: Promoting Fairness

In applying AI to high-stakes social domains like hiring, lending and policing, a real danger exists that algorithms could perpetuate and scale historic biases rather than mitigate them. However, biases infiltrate at multiple levels.

Flawed or unrepresentative training data and myopic performance metrics frequently introduce discrimination. But ingrained human prejudices also complicate uncovering unfairness. Thoughtful statistical techniques, auditing processes, and inclusive teams empower unravelling biases challenging to spot otherwise. Law and regulation establishing oversight of algorithmic systems provide additional safeguards.

Yet frameworks for AI fairness remain debated, as equal representation mathematically does not guarantee equitable treatment socially. Navigating bias requires acknowledging hard truths on the uneven playing fields algorithms are deployed into. There are rarely easy technical fixes to systemic injustices, but we can bend the arc of progress through integrity.

- AI Regulation and Governance

As algorithms shape vital social functions, calls for governance frameworks balancing innovation, safety, and ethics grow louder. However, regulating rapidly evolving technologies comes with challenges. Premature or inflexible laws stifle progress, while inaction breeds public mistrust.

Most experts recommend sector-specific accountability standards over-generalized laws. Creating dedicated public oversight bodies also fosters transparency on privacy, autonomy and acceptable use. Global coordination on principles helps unite efforts across borders.

But living up to ethical ideals requires perseverance. We must prudently assess how to nurture AI for social benefit without presuming perfection. Thoughtful cooperation across government, companies and civil society can help ensure AI systems reflect shared values even as capabilities advance.

- AI and Philosophy: The Search for Machine Morality

At its deepest levels, debates on AI's social impacts raise philosophical questions about ethics, human identity, and the nature of intelligence. Some posit AI as an existential threat to humanity. But such fears often reflect hubristic assumptions of achieving artificial general intelligence surpassing people.

Alternatively, humanistic philosophies argue for uplifting human dignity and wisdom alongside technological progress. Rather than perfection, AI offers lessons in our shared fallibility. And calls for robot rights seem less urgent than ensuring justice for everyone first. Straightforward ethical values like honesty, compassion and solidarity may ground AI more than pursuing artificial sentience.

No consensus exists on machine morality. But inclusive discourse bridging diverse perspectives offers promise. We need not agree on far-flung futures to make incremental progress in implementing ethics where we can today.

- Towards an AI Ethics Toolkit

While primary open debates remain, practitioners can still take pragmatic steps to align AI products with ethical purposes:

- Conduct fairness and risk reviews exploring potential harms before deployment.
- Build diverse teams with interdisciplinary perspectives to uncover blind spots.
- Implement fairness toolkits and bias bounties to surface discrimination through continuous testing.
- Adopt secure computing techniques like encryption and access controls to protect users.
- Create feedback loops allowing monitoring systems and correcting errors over time.
- Establish ethics advisory boards, external audits, and whistleblower policies to ensure accountability.
- Document processes and data sources for explainability, not just performance metrics.
- Set up grievance redressal mechanisms for affected communities.
- Share best practices openly to raise industry standards collectively.

These steps demonstrate how organizations can cultivate internal cultures fostering ethical AI within current constraints. The journey continues through committed cooperation.

- The Future We Shape Together

Grappling with the societal impacts of AI compels us to reflect deeply on justice, humanity and progress. There are no perfect answers. But through compassion and moral courage, we can build a common cause to guide AI toward creating more opportunity than disruption.

Technology doesn't develop independently of human values; it reflects them. The future remains unwritten, awaiting the choices we make today. We can realize AI's promise while addressing its perils by lifting each other, not just metrics. We can forge an intelligent society in harmony with our ideals with diligence and empathy. The task begins now through working hand in hand.

CHAPTER THIRTEEN

CONCLUSION: EMBRACING OUR AI FUTURE

Our journey exploring the world of artificial intelligence nears its end. We uncovered AI's technical building blocks in these pages, from machine learning to neural networks. We surveyed remarkable applications already transforming fields from healthcare to transportation. We had frank discussions on the profound opportunities and risks AI's rise entails for society.

Synthesizing these threads, four key lessons warrant emphasis as takeaways:

- Lesson 1: AI is Here - Subtly, Messily, Powerfully

The AI systems transforming our digital lives bear little resemblance to the superintelligent robots of science fiction. But in messy, mundane, and profound ways, this technology has already become pervasive by quietly weaving itself into the fabric of society.

We interact with AI daily through apps, assistants, recommendations, and optimized logistics. But capabilities remain bounded within narrow domains; advanced as algorithms grow, their brittle nature remains apparent. However, dismissing AI's messy potency is unwise simply because cosmic ambitions remain unrealized.

- Lesson 2: AI is Human - Embodying Our Hopes and Faults

AI may power autonomous machines, but it originates from human minds and hands. At its essence, AI reflects creators' goals - for better or worse. But human values differ; we diverge on ethics, justice, and rights.

So, while engineering objective AI is seductive, true neutrality does not exist. Trade-offs emerge on matters from privacy to accountability. But this connection means AI's course depends on our collective choices. Its future need not be fixed but can be consciously shaped.

- Lesson 3: AI is Hard - Requiring Wisdom and Nuance

For all the hype, creating AI that broadly mimics human cognition remains incredibly difficult. Noisy data, biased algorithms, brittle systems, inadequate computing, ethical blindspots - obstacles litter the path ahead. There are no shortcuts to the mastery we wish machines to demonstrate.

Thus, wisdom is required in pacing unsteady progress, tempering expectations, and questioning motives. The roadmap must balance undisciplined innovation with lax indifference, as each enables different harms. But if navigated prudently, step-by-step, AI can uplift society with care and nuance.

- Lesson 4: AI is Hope - Turning Intelligence into Insight

Notwithstanding current limits, AI represents immense hope. In areas from medicine to education, sustainability to equality, this technology can unlock insights and efficiencies, improving lives if developed ethically.

But ultimately, machines alone cannot resolve our most profound challenges without broader cooperation and justice. Progress emerges through original algorithms, open minds, and good faith in equal measure. By lifting each other and asking AI to amplify our shared truths rather than individual triumphs, a brighter future awaits.

- Navigating Our AI Moment as One

What next steps should we take together? Three priorities stand out:

- First, continue demystifying AI through education and open discourse - a public empowered by an understanding of this technology's realities and risks is society's sharpest safeguard.
- Second, intentionally guide the development and application of AI toward humanitarian ends like sustainable development, healthcare access, and opportunity creation to harness its benefits responsibly.
- And finally, cultivate multi-stakeholder partnerships bridging the public, private, and research sectors. Progress arises through good-faith cooperation, balancing innovation with ethics.

The years ahead promise to challenge our institutions, beliefs, and identities. But by embracing humanity in technology, rather than ceding ground to faceless systems, we can author an uplifting story for the age of artificial intelligence.

As we conclude, remember that the future remains unwritten. Our machines need not control us, nor we them.

Together, with care and courage, let us welcome AI as an opportunity to better ourselves and our societies.

*"Many unknowns persist on the road ahead, but the destination can still be hopeful - if we make the journey with empathy and solidarity with one another." - **Dr Shahrukh Khan.***

Artificial Intelligence – Historical Timeline

Chronology highlights critical milestones in the history and evolution of artificial intelligence, which I feel you have to know to understand the development of AI.

Ancient Philosophical Beginnings

1. Antiquity: The seeds of AI are sown in ancient Greek philosophy with the concept of automatons, intelligent mechanical beings.
2. 13th Century: The Arabic polymath Al-Jazari designs a humanoid automaton.
3. 17th Century: René Descartes introduces the idea of animal-like machines.

Emergence of Computing

1. 19th Century: George Boole's work on symbolic logic lays the foundation for modern computer science.
2. 1936: Alan Turing introduces the concept of a theoretical universal machine known as the Turing Machine.
3. 1941: Konrad Zuse builds the Z3, the world's first electromechanical, programmable computer.

Birth of AI

1. 1950: Alan Turing proposes the Turing Test to assess a machine's ability to exhibit intelligent behaviour.
2. 1956: Dartmouth Workshop marks the birth of AI as a field with John McCarthy coining the term.
3. 1960s: AI research receives significant funding from the U.S. government.
4. 1965: Joseph Weizenbaum developed ELIZA, an early natural language processing program

AI Winters and Revival

1. The 1970s: AI research faced setbacks, leading to the first AI winter.
2. The 1980s: Expert systems and rule-based AI gained popularity.
3. 1983: Rodney Brooks developed the subsumption architecture for robotics.
4. The 1990s: AI enters the mainstream with applications like chess-playing programs and internet search engines.

The Machine Learning Revolution

1. 1997: IBM's Deep Blue defeats Garry Kasparov in a historic chess match.
2. The 2000s: Machine learning and neural networks advance rapidly.
3. 2011: IBM's Watson wins Jeopardy! against human champions.
4. 2012: The deep learning revolution begins with Geoffrey Hinton's success in image classification.

The Modern AI Era

1. 2016: AlphaGo, developed by DeepMind, defeats world champion Go player Lee Sedol.
2. 2017: AI-powered personal assistants like Siri and Alexa become household names.
3. 2020: GPT-3, the most prominent language model yet, is unveiled by OpenAI.
4. 2020s: AI transforms industries, from healthcare and finance to self-driving cars and entertainment.

Now that we've journeyed through the chronology of AI let's explore the key concepts and terms in our glossary to ensure you have a comprehensive understanding of this exciting field.

Glossary

In our exploration of Artificial Intelligence (AI), it's essential to clarify the terminology that underpins this dynamic field. This glossary will serve as your compass, helping you navigate the intricate landscape of AI concepts and jargon.

1. Artificial Intelligence (AI): A branch of computer science that focuses on creating machines capable of performing tasks that typically require human intelligence, such as learning, reasoning, problem-solving, and language understanding.
2. Machine Learning (ML): A subset of AI that empowers machines to improve their performance on a task through experience and data without being explicitly programmed.
3. Deep Learning: A type of machine learning inspired by the structure and function of the human brain, utilizing neural networks with multiple layers to process data and make decisions.
4. Neural Network: A computational model inspired by the human brain's structure, composed of interconnected nodes (neurons) that process information through layers of computation.
5. Algorithm: A set of rules and instructions designed to solve a problem or perform a particular task.
6. Data Science: The field that involves collecting, analyzing, and interpreting large volumes of data to extract valuable insights and patterns.
7. Natural Language Processing (NLP): A branch of AI that focuses on enabling machines to understand, interpret, and generate human language.
8. Computer Vision: A field within AI that teaches computers to interpret and understand visual information from the world, often using image and video data.
9. Reinforcement Learning: A machine learning approach where agents learn to make sequences of decisions by receiving

feedback as rewards or penalties.

10. Turing Test: A test proposed by Alan Turing to assess a machine's ability to exhibit human-like intelligence, typically in natural language conversation.

11. Chatbot: A computer program designed to simulate human conversation, often used for customer service or interactive tasks.

12. Big Data: Huge and complex datasets that require advanced computational and analytical techniques to extract meaningful information.

13. Internet of Things (IoT): A network of interconnected physical devices and objects communicating and sharing data over the internet.

14. Algorithm Bias: When machine learning algorithms produce unfair or discriminatory results due to biased training data or flawed design.

15. Ethical AI: The practice of developing and using AI in a manner that aligns with moral principles, respecting privacy, transparency, and fairness.

16. Singularity: A hypothetical future point at which AI may surpass human intelligence, potentially leading to profound societal changes.

17. Bias Mitigation: Strategies and techniques used to reduce or eliminate bias in AI algorithms, ensuring fairness and equity.

18. AI Ethics: The study of moral and ethical issues related to the development and use of AI technology, including accountability, transparency, and responsibility.

19. AI Integration: Incorporating AI technology into various industries and sectors, from healthcare and finance to transportation and entertainment.

20. Quantum Computing: A cutting-edge computing technology that leverages the principles of quantum mechanics to perform complex calculations at unprecedented speeds.

21. Robotics: The intersection of AI, engineering and computer science to create intelligent mechanical agents that can perceive,

reason, manipulate and move independently within the physical world.

22. Algorithmic Bias: Errors, prejudices or discrimination propagated through AI algorithms that can negatively impact certain user groups and outcomes. They are typically introduced via flawed training data, poor model design, or unethical applications.

23. Singularity: The theoretical point at which artificial intelligence exceeds human intellectual capacity, with profound implications. Views vary widely on if/when this could feasibly occur.

24. Superintelligence: A hypothesized form of artificial intelligence surpassing human-level general intelligence in almost all domains of cognitive capability.

As we wrap up our glossary, remember that these terms are the foundation of your AI journey. They will guide you through the intricacies of this ever-evolving field, ensuring you grasp the nuances of the concepts discussed throughout this book.

Author's Note

Dear Reader,

If you've made it to these final pages, thank you for joining me in exploring the promising yet complex world of artificial intelligence. I am filled with gratitude and a profound sense of accomplishment as we reach the final pages of our journey through Artificial Intelligence.

When I started writing, I intended to demystify AI and make this complex subject accessible to everyone. I set out to lift the veil shrouding AI for many people unfamiliar with the technical details or business contexts behind phrases like "machine learning" or "neural networks" that we often hear today. I hoped to give you - the curious citizen, the business leader, the policymaker - a window into this rapidly evolving field so you can engage thoughtfully in discussions about our automated present and future.

Inaccessible hype and fearmongering dominate too much public discourse on AI. I strived to cut through these extremes with a balanced guide firmly grounded in today's systems' realities, capabilities, and limitations. But I also aimed to convey an appreciation for how far artificial intelligence has come in decades while prompting reflective conversations about where it still needs to go responsibly.

If reading this book sparked new perspectives on how AI is shaping and being shaped by society, I accomplished my goal. My deepest hope is to provide a valuable foundation to think critically about AI's implications and our shared responsibility in steering it wisely.

As we conclude this journey, I want to emphasize that the road ahead will have many twists and turns. AI's capabilities will continue to grow in the coming years, and we must stay engaged with developments through learning, discussing, and actively contributing to progress in our communities. The destination can still be one of hope and uplifting humanity if we travel together.

It is not technology alone but how we choose to wield it that will determine whether AI enables or inhibits human flourishing. Thank you for reading and for playing a part in shaping our collective future.

With heartfelt thanks,
Dr. Shahrukh Khan

Acknowledgments

As we close the final chapter of this book, I would be remiss not to express my deep gratitude to the individuals and institutions that have made this journey possible.

First and foremost, I want to acknowledge the countless researchers, scientists, engineers, and visionaries who have dedicated their lives to Artificial Intelligence. Your tireless pursuit of knowledge and innovation has paved the way for the incredible advancements we've explored in these pages.

I owe a debt of gratitude to my colleagues, mentors, and friends who generously shared their insights and expertise. Your guidance and support have been invaluable in shaping the content of this book.

I extend my heartfelt thanks to my family (My Dad, Mother and Kiddo Sister), whose unwavering support and encouragement sustained me through the writing process. Your belief in this project fueled my determination to make AI accessible to a broader audience.

A special note of appreciation goes to the dedicated team at our publishing house, whose commitment to excellence transformed my words into a cohesive narrative. Your dedication to the craft of storytelling has brought this book to life.

To the readers who have embarked on this journey with me, thank you for your curiosity, time, and engagement. Your presence on this expedition has been the most rewarding aspect of this endeavour.

And finally, to the future generations who will inherit the legacy of AI, I implore you to approach this field with a sense of wonder and responsibility. The possibilities are boundless, and the burden is significant. May you continue to push the boundaries of knowledge and wield AI's power for the betterment of humanity.

With heartfelt appreciation,

Dr. Shahrukh Khan